Superstructures

INCREDIBLE
SKYSCRAPERS

Geoff Barker

amicus

mankato, minnesota

Published by Amicus
P.O. Box 1329, Mankato, Minnesota 56002

Printed in the United States of America at Corporate Graphics, in North Mankato, Minnesota.

Published by arrangement with the Watts Publishing Group Ltd., London.

Library of Congress Cataloging-in-Publication Data
Barker, Geoff P., 1963-
  Incredible skyscrapers / by Geoff Barker.
      p. cm. -- (Superstructures)
  Summary: "Describes some of the tallest and most famous skyscrapers ever built. Includes information on the architects, the challenges they faced, and statistics of the finished skyscrapers"--Provided by publisher.
  Includes index.
  ISBN 978-1-60753-133-3 (library binding)
  1. Skyscrapers--Juvenile literature. I. Title.
  TH1615.B37 2011
  720'.483--dc22
                                            2009044044

Editor: Michael Downey
Art Direction: Harleen Mehta (Q2AMedia)
Designer: Tarang Saggar (Q2AMedia)
Picture Researcher: Kamal Kumar (Q2AMedia)
Illustrators: Sibi ND and Danish Zaidi (Q2AMedia)

Picture credits:
t=top b=bottom c=center l=left r=right

Cover: Jose Fuste Raga/ Age fotostock/ Photolibrary: Front, Ng Wei Keong/ Shutterstock: Back

Title Page: Lynn Watson/ Shutterstock

Underwood & Underwood/ Corbis: 4, Michael S. Yamashita/ Corbis: 5br, Kated/ Shutterstock: 6, George Fischer/ CN Tower: 7b, Index Stock Imagery/ Photolibrary: 8, Lynn Watson/ Shutterstock: 10, Jon Arnold/ Photolibrary: 12, Layne Kennedy/ Corbis: 13, Bartlomiej Magierowski/ 123rf: 14, Jose Fuste Raga/ Age fotostock/ Photolibrary: 15, Max Romeo/ Shutterstock: 16, Jose Fuste Raga/ Corbis: 17tl, Bill Croson: 18, Jose Fuste Raga/ Corbis: 19, Mike Kemp/ Corbis: 20t, Fritz Hoffmann/ Corbis: 21, Sylvain Grandadam/ Age fotostock/ Photolibrary: 22, Superstock/ Photolibrary: 23tl, Michele Falzone/ Jon Arnold Travel/ Photolibrary: 24, Louie Psihoyos/ Corbis: 25tr, Teo Huai Wei Edmund: 25b, Emaar Properties: 26, Skidmore, Owings & Merrill LLP/ Renew NYC/ LMDC: 28, Madinat al-Hareer: 29.

Q2AMedia Art Bank: 5tl, 7tr, 9, 11, 17b, 20bl, 27t, 27b.

Note to parents and teachers:
Every effort has been made by the publishers to ensure that the web sites in this book are suitable for children, that they are of the highest educational value, and that they contain no inappropriate or offensive material.
However, because of the nature of the Internet, it is impossible to guarantee that the contents of these sites will not be altered. We strongly advise that Internet access is supervised by a responsible adult.

1210
32010

9 8 7 6 5 4 3 2 1

CONTENTS

EARLY SKYSCRAPERS

We think of skyscrapers as modern, tall buildings with office space to house thousands of city workers. But many centuries ago, people also built tall, impressive buildings. Among these were massive stone churches with tall **spires** and **steeples** that stretched high into the sky. Today's skyscrapers rise even higher, and some really do seem to touch the sky!

Steel Revolution

The start of modern steelmaking in 1858 made the building of the first skyscrapers possible. During the nineteenth-century **Industrial Revolution**, huge quantities of **steel** were made. This light, but strong, metal made a difference in how large buildings were constructed.

First Skyscraper

The Home Insurance Building in Chicago is often thought to be the world's first skyscraper. Built in 1885, this early giant was originally 10 floors high. Two more floors were added in 1890. It was demolished in 1931 to make way for another building.

*Built of **cast** and **wrought iron**, Chicago's Home Insurance Building also included steel in its frame structure. If it had been built of stone, it would have weighed three times more.*

STEEL SKELETON

The science of skyscrapers is simple. Putting one floor on top of another is like stacking square wooden blocks on top of each other. The more blocks you add, the more wobbly the structure becomes. To stand up against strong winds, early skyscrapers used a strong steel skeleton of **vertical columns** and **horizontal beams** that were bolted together.

Horizontal beam

Vertical column

Wedge-Shaped Building

The distinctive 285-foot (87 m) tall Fuller Building in New York City, built between 1901 and 1903, is an example of an early skyscraper. Although not as tall as modern skyscrapers, it is still one of the most photographed landmarks in New York City. Commonly known as the Flatiron Building, it fits snugly into a tight triangular space between two of Manhattan's main avenues.

New York City's Flatiron Building is wedged between Broadway and Fifth Avenue.

TOWER OR SKYSCRAPER?

A skyscraper is an extremely tall building. There are some towers, however, that are even taller than skyscrapers. What is the difference between a skyscraper and a tower? Skyscrapers are buildings where people either live or work, or both. Towers are not places for people to live or work in.

Eiffel Tower

One of the world's most famous towers is France's Eiffel Tower (right). Designed by Gustave Eiffel, the tower was completed in time for the 1889 World's Fair in Paris. Made from wrought iron, it reached a height of 984 feet (300 m). This made it the world's tallest structure at that time.

AMAZING FACTS

From 1889 to 1931, France's Eiffel Tower held the record as the world's tallest tower.

More than 200 million people have visited the Eiffel Tower since its **construction**.

In 1995, the American Society of **Civil Engineers** voted the CN Tower to be one of the seven modern wonders of the world.

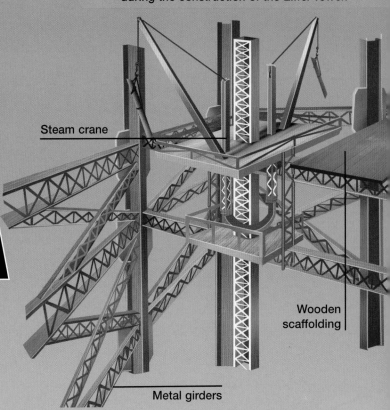

Small, steam-powered cranes were used during the construction of the Eiffel Tower.

Steam crane

Wooden scaffolding

Metal girders

Taller and Taller

At 1,814 feet (553 m) high, the CN Tower in Toronto, Canada, was the world's tallest tower for more than three decades. Its main pod contains a revolving restaurant and observation gallery, which visitors reach by high-speed elevators. This massive tower is now dwarfed by the 2,064-foot (629 m) KVLY-TV mast near Fargo in North Dakota. The KVLY-TV **transmission antenna** is held in place by strong **guy lines**.

An elegant nighttime lighting system was added to Canada's CN Tower.

EMPIRE STATE BUILDING

Number 350, Fifth Avenue, New York City, is better known as the Empire State Building. This early skyscraper was built in 1931 and is world famous. In the film *King Kong*, the giant, rampaging gorilla climbed the building, only to be shot at from an airplane and killed. The Empire State Building was the tallest building in the world for 41 years. In 1972, however, it was overtaken by New York's World Trade Center.

What's in a Name?

The Empire State Building's name comes from a nickname for New York City. It used to be known as the Empire City, located in the so-called Empire State of New York. Shortly after the Empire State Building was built, the United States suffered a severe **economic depression**. As there were very few new **tenants**, the building was called the Empty State Building as a joke by New Yorkers.

FACT FILE
- Height: 1,250 ft. (381 m)
- Where in the world: New York City, New York
- When built: 1931
- Designed by: Shreve, Lamb and Harmon Associates
- Materials used: Steel, limestone, and granite

New York's Empire State Building contains about 10 million bricks.

Pavement Attraction

As many as 25,000 people work in the skyscraper, which is also a major tourist attraction. More than 120 million people have visited the viewing galleries on the 86th and 102nd floors. One of its greatest fans was French **architect** Le Corbusier. He said, "I could lie on the pavement and look at it forever."

Dominating the Skyline

The Empire State Building is 1,250 feet (381 m) tall. With its extended tower, it is 1,476 feet (450 m) high. Currently, it is the tallest building in New York. But the Willis Tower in Chicago is the tallest skyscraper in the United States.

AMAZING FACTS

Construction work on the Empire State Building began in 1930, when 200 steel and **concrete piles**, or columns, were driven 36 feet (11 m) into the ground to sit on the granite bedrock.

As many as 3,400 workers were on site at the same time during the building of the Empire State Building.

This early skyscraper was built ahead of schedule in a short amount of time. It took just one year and 45 days to complete.

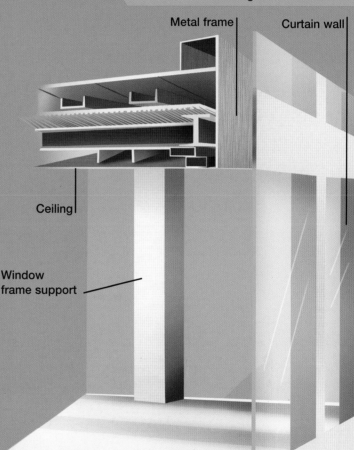

The curtain wall protects the building from the weather.

Metal frame

Curtain wall

Ceiling

Window frame support

CURTAIN WALL

A building's curtain wall is not intended to support the building's weight. Instead, the skyscraper's outer wall covers the building's frame and protects people inside from the weather. The Art Deco exterior of the Empire State Building is made of limestone and granite panels. Like the curtain wall on many modern skyscrapers, this outer layer is also used for decoration. A number of modern skyscrapers have a curtain

WILLIS TOWER

Chicago's Willis Tower became the world's highest building in 1973 and kept this record for nearly 25 years. In a city of high-rise structures, this gigantic skyscraper dominates the skyline. Originally called Sears Tower, the skyscraper was designed by a talented team of architects and engineers from the city of Chicago. The designers understood the problems of this famous Windy City, with average wind speeds of 15.5 miles (25 km) per hour.

Willis Tower's two huge antennas flash to warn passing low aircraft.

FACT FILE
- Height: 1,450 ft. (442 m)
- Where in the world: Chicago, Illinois
- When built: 1973
- Designed by: Skidmore, Owings and Merrill
- Materials used: Steel with black aluminum exterior

Fierce Winds

Willis Tower was designed to be 82 feet (25 m) taller than New York City's World Trade Center's Tower 1, which was the world's tallest skyscraper at that time. Its architects had to design a building that was not only tall, but one that could withstand Chicago's fiercest winds. Like the World Trade Center's famous Twin Towers, Willis Tower was to become a successful example of **tube building** design.

Four cross sections of Sears Tower show the way floors are laid out at different levels of the Chicago skyscraper.

Floor 110

Floor 90

Floor 66

Floor 50

AMAZING FACTS

In 1999, famous French urban climber Alain "Spiderman" Robert successfully climbed, without equipment, Willis Tower's glassy front.

From the Visitor Skydeck, you can see Illinois and three other states—Indiana, Michigan, and Wisconsin.

Six machines are mounted on top of the Willis Tower roof to clean its 16,000 windows.

There is enough steel in the tower to build 50,000 cars.

TUBE BUILDINGS

The type of skyscraper known as a tube building is built with huge columns and beams that are placed close together in the outer walls to form the frame of the building. The rigid outer walls make the entire building, in effect, a huge hollow tube. This has proved to be a very efficient design for a skyscraper. Willis Tower has a bundle of nine square steel tubes that form extremely rigid columns with floors suspended inside the columns. The design narrows in steps as the building rises, and this helps to reduce the wind forces higher up the building.

Improving Reception

In 1982, two television antennas were added
to the roof of the tower. In 2000, one antenna
was extended to 283 feet (86 m) to improve
TV **reception**, giving Willis Tower a total height
of 1,729 feet (527 m). Due to their height and
position on the Chicago skyline, the antennas
are often hit by lightning.

Television Antenna

Although the tallest television antenna on
the Willis Tower stretches high above its
roof, it is not included in the building's total
height. Spires count toward the height of
a skyscraper. Unfortunately for the Chicago
landmark, radio and television antennas do
not. The Willis Tower is no longer the world's
tallest skyscraper. However, it is still the
tallest in the United States.

SOLID BEDROCK

The Willis Tower architects had more than
strong wind forces to think about when they
designend the skyscraper. As the building
weighs 220,462 tons (200,000 t), it also
needed extremely strong **foundations**. To
get this strength, 114 piles, or steel and
concrete columns, were sunk deep into the
ground using powerful machines called
piledrivers. The specially strengthened
concrete columns had to stand firmly on
the solid bedrock to hold up the structure.
Without these, the tall skyscraper would
have started to sink into the ground under

Light in Comparison

Using steel in the Willis Tower was very economical. Only 248 pounds of steel per square yard (135 kg per square meter) were needed during its construction. More traditional skyscrapers with supporting columns use more than 368 pounds of steel per square yard (200 kg per square meter). Willis Tower compares favorably with more modern structures. Less than 77,161 tons (70,000 t) of steel were used, and the building weighs only 220,462 tons (200,000 t) in total. This is less than one third of the total weight of Taiwan's Taipei 101 skyscraper (see pages 24–25).

Using Sky Lobbies

As many as 25,000 people travel up and down Willis Tower every working day. The company that designed the elevator system for Willis Tower used areas known as **sky lobbies** to keep things flowing. Sky lobbies are special floors in which people can wait and change elevators. In Willis Tower, these lobbies are on floors 33/34 and 66/67. Here, people board and get off double-decker express elevators. From the sky lobbies, people can take any of the slower elevators serving individual floors to reach their final destination.

The Willis Tower's observation decks provide stunning views over Chicago's cityscape.

SHUN HING SQUARE

Twenty years ago, Shenzhen was the tiny Chinese village of Bao'an. The Chinese government invested in the region and Shenzhen was built in its place. At 1,260 feet (384 m), Shenzhen's Shun Hing Square became the city's tallest skyscraper. When built, it was the tallest building outside the United States. It was soon overtaken by China's CITIC Plaza and Malaysia's Petronas Towers.

FACT FILE

- Height: 1,260 feet (384 m)
- Where in the world: Shenzhen, China
- When built: 1996
- Designed by: K Y Cheung Design Associates
- Materials: Steel, glass, concrete

Shun Hing Square towers above other buildings in China's Shenzhen City.

Skyscraper City

Shenzhen's skyline was recently voted as the fifth best in the world. The city has more than 20 buildings higher than 656 feet (200 m) and more are going up every year. The Kingkey Finance Tower, which will be completed in 2010, will be 1,440 feet (439 m) in height.

Distinctive Spires

Shun Hing Square is a complex that serves different purposes. The main 69-floor office tower, with its two distinctive spires, has a public viewing gallery on its top floor. There is a separate 35-floor building with offices, apartments, and a five-**story** shopping center. Although Shun Hing Square is tall, it measures only 1,066 feet (325 m) without its spires. Its highest occupied floor is 978 feet (298 m) above the ground.

Typhoon-Proof Tower

The main office building of Shun Hing Square, known as Di Wang Tower, has a steel frame constructed of vertical columns and horizontal beams. It also has a **core** of **reinforced** concrete. In September 1999, **Typhoon** York swept across Hong Kong and Shenzhen. Although this typhoon had the highest warning level and lasted for 11 hours, Di Wang Tower's strong construction enabled it to survive the typhoon.

AMAZING FACTS

The total floor area of Shun Hing Square is equal to 67 acres (27 hectares)!

Shun Hing Square is the tallest steel-framed building in China.

During construction, four floors were built in just nine days.

15

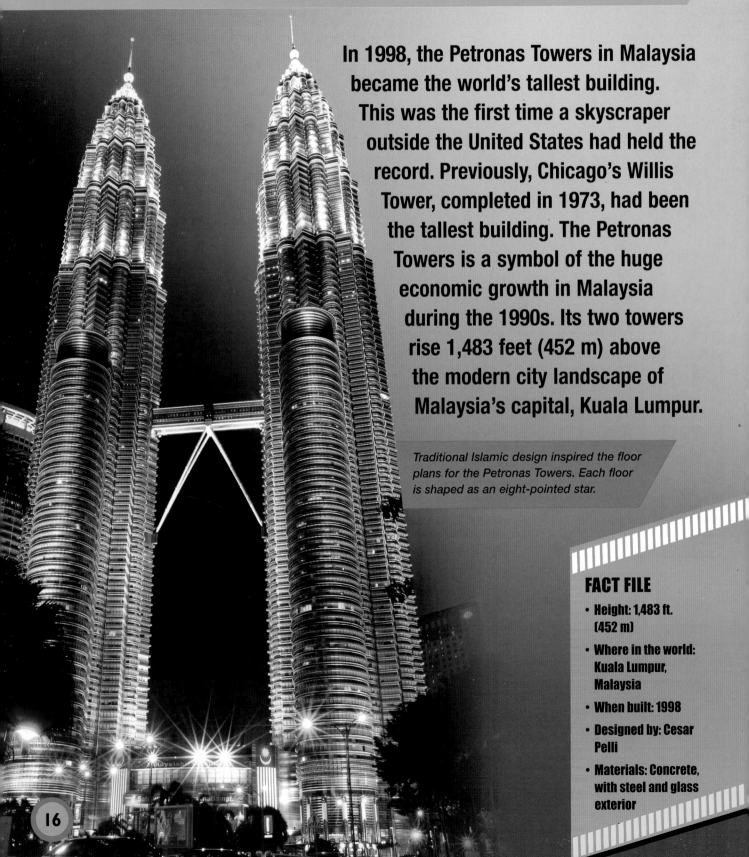

PETRONAS TOWERS

In 1998, the Petronas Towers in Malaysia became the world's tallest building. This was the first time a skyscraper outside the United States had held the record. Previously, Chicago's Willis Tower, completed in 1973, had been the tallest building. The Petronas Towers is a symbol of the huge economic growth in Malaysia during the 1990s. Its two towers rise 1,483 feet (452 m) above the modern city landscape of Malaysia's capital, Kuala Lumpur.

Traditional Islamic design inspired the floor plans for the Petronas Towers. Each floor is shaped as an eight-pointed star.

FACT FILE

- Height: 1,483 ft. (452 m)
- Where in the world: Kuala Lumpur, Malaysia
- When built: 1998
- Designed by: Cesar Pelli
- Materials: Concrete, with steel and glass exterior

Petronas Towers' main elevator systems are located in the center of each tower.

Bridge in the Sky

The two Petronas Towers are connected by a **flexible** bridge at the 41st and 42nd floors. This sky bridge is 33 feet (10 m) tall and 197 feet (60 m) long. It was built in South Korea and put together on the ground at the construction site in Kuala Lumpur. The 716.5 ton (650 t) bridge had to be lifted to a height of 604 feet (184 m).

Leaning Tower

One of the difficulties in building Petronas Towers was that a different construction company was used to build each tower. A Japanese company, Hazama Corporation, worked on Tower 1. South Korean builders worked on Tower 2. While Hazama spent valuable time finding a solution to Tower 1 leaning 1 inch (2.5 cm), the South Korean construction team was able to complete Tower 2 successfully.

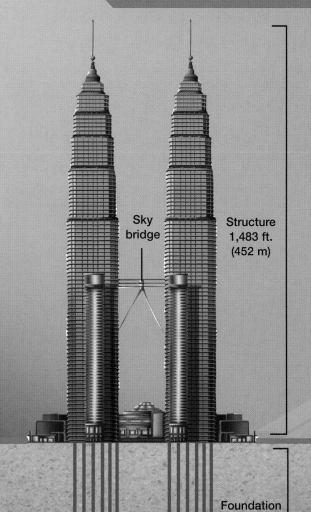

Sky bridge

Structure 1,483 ft. (452 m)

Foundation 394 ft. (120 m)

Bedrock

Malaysia's twin towers were built on the world's deepest foundations to balance their great height.

AMAZING FACTS

Without any stops, it takes just 90 seconds to go up the Petronas Towers by elevator from the basement to the top of either tower.

The towers were featured in the 1999 film *Entrapment*, starring Catherine Zeta-Jones and Sean Connery.

There are about 16,000 windows in each tower. It takes a month to wash each tower, after which it is time to clean the windows again!

JIN MAO BUILDING

The Jin Mao Building, which means Golden Prosperity Building, rises high above Shanghai's skyline. Based on the style of Chinese **pagodas**, the building's **tiers** gradually taper inward and floors become smaller toward the top. This building is one of the first of China's immense towers.

FACT FILE

- Height: 1,381 ft. (421 m)
- Where in the world: Shanghai, China
- When built: 1999
- Designed by: Adrian Smith; Skidmore, Owings and Merrill
- Materials: Steel and concrete

The structure of Jin Mao Building becomes more complex as it rises.

World's Highest Hotel

The Jin Mao Building has 88 floors. There are shops and restaurants, and floors 3 to 50 are used for office space. The Jin Mao Building is also the world's tallest building containing a hotel. The five-star Grand Hyatt Hotel, which occupies the top 38 floors, has the highest hotel rooms in the world!

Elevators Inside and Outside

It is not practical for a high-rise building to be serviced solely by stairs. People need elevators. In skyscrapers, elevators are usually situated in the central part of the building. The Jin Mao Building's elevators and staircases are in the eight-sided inner vertical passage that rises from the ground to floor 53. The upper floors, occupied by the Grand Hyatt Hotel's 555 rooms, are serviced by elevators that glide up and down the outside of the **structural** inner core.

Jin Mao Building (center) is a key feature of Shanghai's dramatic skyline.

LUCKY NUMBER EIGHT

In China, the number eight is considered to be very lucky. This number crops up everywhere in the construction and design of the Jin Mao Building, which has 88 floors! The building's inner core of eight enormous columns acts like a spine for a skeleton. The concrete columns are surrounded by eight columns of steel that help the skyscraper withstand powerful typhoons and earthquakes.

19

Spiraling corridors

Structural inner core

Elevators

*The massive **atrium** in the Jin Mao Building rises from the 56th floor to the 87th floor. It is lined with spiraling corridors and staircases.*

How Does a Damper Work?

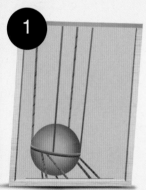

Damper sways left, counteracting a building's movement to the right

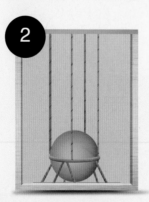

Damper is at the midpoint of its swaying motion

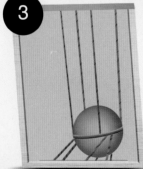

Damper sways right, counteracting a building's movement to the left

Counteracting Sway

The Jin Mao Building was designed to survive extreme weather conditions without suffering damage. The tower can withstand typhoon winds and powerful earthquakes. The Grand Hyatt Hotel's swimming pool on the 57th floor serves a vital function. Apart from providing entertainment for the hotel guests, the pool also acts as a **damper** to help reduce wind movement. A damper is a heavy weight that works to **counteract** the swaying of a building. As the Jin Mao Building starts to **sway** one way, the weight of the swimming pool makes the building move more slowly. In effect, it pulls the tower back toward the center. This limits the movement of the entire building.

High-Rise Tragedy

A huge skyscraper presents one of the biggest challenges to extreme sports enthusiasts. Famous urban climber Alain "Spiderman" Robert successfully scaled the Jin Mao Building in 2007. Tragically, BASE jumper Roland "Slim" Simpson from Australia died following a jump from the top of the building in 2003. BASE is short for Buildings, Antennas, Spans (bridges), and Earth (cliffs). Jumpers use a parachute or a "wing suit" and a parachute. In the jump from the Jin Mao Building, Simpson's parachute did not open properly.

Construction workers on the Jin Mao Building needed a head for heights and steady feet.

AMAZING FACTS

The Jin Mao Building has the world's longest **laundry chute**. It runs from the top of the tower to the basement. Buffers along its length slow down the speed of falling laundry.

In 2001, 31-year-old shoe salesman Han Qizhi was the first person to scale the Jin Mao Building.

2IFC, HONG KONG

Architect Cesar Pelli won an international competition to design Tower 2 of the International Finance Centre, or 2IFC for short, in the heart of the city of Hong Kong. Strong and elegant at 1,362 feet (415 m), 2IFC dwarfs 1IFC, which is 689 feet (210 m) high. With 88 floors, 2IFC currently is Hong Kong's tallest building.

FACT FILE

- **Height:** 1,362 ft. (415 m)
- **Where in the world:** Hong Kong, China
- **When built:** 2003
- **Designed by:** Cesar Pelli
- **Materials:** Steel and glass

Square Central Core

The 2IFC was built in record time. Its 88 floors were built at a rate of one every three days. The building's structure is straightforward, which helped to speed up construction. 2IFC has a huge, square central core made from reinforced concrete. This supports the structure like a strong backbone. To strengthen the core, there are eight steel and concrete columns and eight smaller steel columns. Seen from above, the supporting columns are arranged in a cross-like formation. The curtain wall is lightweight and provides minimal support for the building. 2IFC was completed and opened in 2003.

Moving People

Double-decker elevators, in which one car is attached to the top of another, are important features in many newer skyscrapers. These double elevators enable passengers on two different floors to move up or down at the same time, increasing the efficiency of the elevator shaft. These work well in buildings where a busy, single elevator would otherwise stop at every floor. For the 2IFC, double-decker elevators also use less inner core space than normal elevators for the same amount of traffic. This frees up more space on each floor for offices.

2IFC has 42 high-speed passenger elevators that operate in seven different zones.

AMAZING FACTS

2IFC was featured in *Dark Knight* and in *Tomb Raider II: The Cradle of Life*. In these two films, the characters Batman, Lara Croft, and Terry Sheridan jump off the building.

An advertisement was put up on the front of 2IFC in 2003. It was 755 feet (230 m) long and covered 50 floors.

TAIPEI 101

Opened on December 31, 2004, Taiwan's Taipei 101 was a fitting place to start the New Year celebrations. At 187 feet (57 m) taller than Petronas Towers in Kuala Lumpur, Malaysia, Taipei 101 became the world's tallest building.

Stick of Bamboo

Taipei 101, which some people think resembles a giant Chinese pagoda, is a stunning high-rise that dwarfs surrounding buildings. The skyscraper's owner, Taipei Financial Center Corporation, compares Taipei 101 to a stick of bamboo. That explains the rugged, tiered effect of the eight wider sections as the building rises. The Chinese consider bamboo to be very strong and flexible.

FACT FILE

- Height: 1,670 ft. (509 m)
- Where in the world: Taipei, Taiwan
- When built: 2004
- Designed by: C Y Lee
- Materials: Steel

AMAZING FACTS

Why the number 101? The building is situated in Taipei's 101 district. It also has 101 floors!

Taipei 101 was the world's first building to break the 1,640 feet (500 m) mark in height.

Taipei 101 contains the world's fastest **ascending** elevator. It can reach the 89th floor in 37 seconds at a speed of 37 miles (60 km) per hour.

When the Wind Blows

An enormous yellow metal ball, weighing 728 tons (660 t), hangs in the middle of the skyscraper's 88th floor. This damper is designed to absorb wind forces and reduce swaying movements during extreme weather conditions. This is important as Taipei 101 is situated in one of the worst earthquake zones in the world. There were weather problems as the building went up. Five people were killed in 2002 when a construction crane fell during an earthquake. Now that Taipei 101 is complete, the damper should help the building withstand the very worst **tremors**, as well as typhoons.

The Taipei 101 has the fastest elevator in the world.

Standing Firm

A tall skyscraper has to be supported by firm foundations. During construction, up to 400 concrete piles, or huge round columns, were sunk into the ground 262 feet (80 m). This was done so that the piles stand firmly on solid bedrock and will not sink.

The massive yellow damper hangs down to the middle of the skyscraper's 88th floor.

Strong cable

BURJ KHALIFA

In July 2007, Burj Khalifa, formerly known as Burj Dubai or Dubai Tower, surpassed Taipei 101 and became the tallest building. Located in Dubai in the United Arab Emirates, this enormous high-rise has broken all the records. In April 2008, Burj Khalifa overtook the KVLY-TV mast in North Dakota to become the tallest artificial structure in the world. Burj Khalifa is 2,717 feet (828 m) high, more than twice the height of New York's Empire State Building.

Living in the Sky

Burj Khalifa has 160 floors suitable for occupation. This includes offices and luxury residences, four swimming pools, restaurants, a fitness suite, an observation deck, and a viewing gallery.

Y-Shaped Structure

Burj Khalifa has a curtain wall made of glass and metal. The glass covers an area of 99,985 square yards (83,600 sq m) out of a total curtain wall area of 133,353 square yards (111,500 sq m). This massive total area is equivalent to 17 soccer fields. The Y-shaped structure of the tower in cross section makes the most of window area and natural light.

FACT FILE

- Height: 2,717 ft. (828 m)
- Where in the world: Dubai, UAE
- When built: 2003–2009
- Designed by: Adrian Smith; Skidmore, Owings and Merrill
- Materials: Reinforced concrete, glass, and steel exterior

The tip of the tower's spire is visible up to 59 miles (95 km) away.

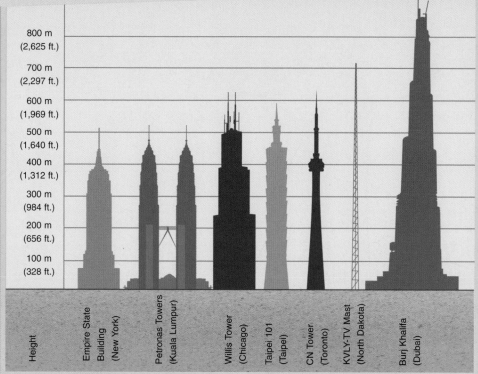

| Height | Empire State Building (New York) | Petronas Towers (Kuala Lumpur) | Willis Tower (Chicago) | Taipei 101 (Taipei) | CN Tower (Toronto) | KVLY-TV Mast (North Dakota) | Burj Khalifa (Dubai) |

800 m (2,625 ft.)
700 m (2,297 ft.)
600 m (1,969 ft.)
500 m (1,640 ft.)
400 m (1,312 ft.)
300 m (984 ft.)
200 m (656 ft.)
100 m (328 ft.)

At more than 2,625 feet (800 m) in height, Burj Khalifa dwarfs other skyscrapers.

Tons of Rebar

In its structure, Burj Khalifa uses **rebar**, which is short for reinforcing bar. Made of steel, rebar is usually formed from a cage or grid of beams that is **embedded** inside concrete. This reinforces the concrete and is stronger than ordinary concrete. The tower, platform, and office annex use 34,613 tons (31,400 t) of rebar. Laid end to end, the steel rebar would stretch more than one quarter of the way around the world!

ADRIAN SMITH

Burj Khalifa's architect, Adrian Smith, has worked for the famous Chicago-based company Skidmore, Owings and Merrill. This top architect also designed the Jin Mao Building. His inspiration for the spectacular design of Burj Khalifa came from a flower called hymenocallis, as well as from traditional patterns in Islamic architecture.

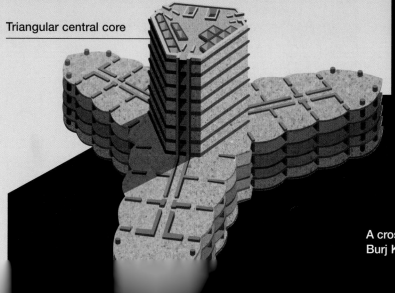

Triangular central core

A cross section of one of Burj Khalifa's lower floors

SKYSCRAPERS IN THE FUTURE

Burj Khalifa is a landmark in the history of high-rise buildings. But many other skyscrapers are being planned, some of which are already underway. Many countries are in friendly competition to build the world's tallest building.

Freedom Tower

New York City is recovering from the destruction in 2001 of the World Trade Center's famous Twin Towers. Work on the foundations of the Freedom Tower, part of the new World Trade Center, began in 2006. Although the new tower will not be the tallest in the world, it will be 1,776 feet (541 m) high. That is 328 feet (100 m) taller than the current tallest U.S. building. The new tower is due to be completed in 2013.

This computer graphic shows how the Freedom Tower will look.

Sky's the Limit

In 2008, Kuwait's government approved plans for a development called Madinat al-Hareer, meaning City of Silk. The centerpiece of the new city will be the Burj Mubarak al-Kabir, a skyscraper reaching a massive 3,284 feet (1,001 m) in height. The futuristic city may take 25 years to build, but the huge tower is set to be completed as early as 2012.

Competing for the Crown

Further proposed mega skyscrapers are the Mile-High Tower in Saudi Arabia and the Murjan Tower in Bahrain. Dubai appears reluctant to give up having the tallest building. Plans are underway to build Al Burj on a site within 15 miles (25 km) of Burj Khalifa. If built, the new skyscraper could be as tall as 4,600 feet (1,400 m).

Burj Mubarak al-Kabir Tower will dominate Kuwait's skyline.

AMAZING FACTS

New York City's Freedom Tower will be 1,776 feet (541 m) tall. This figure reflects the importance of the year 1776 when the American Declaration of Independence was signed.

The Mile-High Tower planned for Jeddah, Saudi Arabia, may not be quite so tall after all. Although it was planned to be 1 mile (1,600 m) tall, the massive skyscraper is more likely to reach 3,610 feet (1,100 m).

GLOSSARY

architect
someone qualified to design buildings and to oversee their construction

Art Deco
distinctive style of decorative art from the 1920s and 1930s

ascending
to be going up

atrium
open hall area inside a building, which may rise up several stories

bedrock
solid layer of rock situated beneath the soil

cast iron
a hard, brittle form of the metal iron

civil engineer
someone qualified to design and construct public works, such as buildings and bridges

concrete
strong building material made using cement, water, and sand or gravel

construction
building or putting up a structure

core
area in the center of a building; strong column surrounding lifts and stairways that supports a skyscraper

counteract
to act against

curtain wall
an outside wall that is not used for support

damper
a heavy weight that helps reduce movement of a tall building during strong winds

economic depression
period when business activity and employment decline severely

embed
fix something firmly into something else

flexible
can be bent easily without breaking

foundations
strong base on which a building stands

granite
hard rock sometimes used by builders

guy lines
ropes or cables used to steady a structure

horizontal beams
strong lengths of metal positioned across a structure for support

Industrial Revolution
transformation of Britain and other countries into industrialized nations

laundry chute
shaft used to send clothes or linens to a lower level

limestone
rock often used for building; also used to make cement

pagoda
tower temple with many tiers or stories

pile
long column hammered vertically into soil to form part of a building's foundation

piledriver
powerful machine used to hammer piles, or strong columns, deep into the ground

rebar
short for "reinforcing bar," a cage or grid of steel beams that is used to make reinforced concrete

reception
in TV or radio, the sound and/or picture quality of a broadcast received

reinforced
strengthened

sky lobby
public area where people wait and change from one set of elevators to another

spire
tall, pointed roof at the top of a tower

steel
strong metal used in building construction

steeple
tall structure at the top of a church or public building, ending with a spire

story
floor or level of a building

structural
to do with the structure, the way a building has been constructed

sway
to swing back and forth

tenants
people who pay to live or work in a building

tier
layer or level

transmission antenna
aerial used for sending radio or TV signals

tremor
minor earthquake

tube building
skyscraper using a system of huge columns to create a hollow tube for support

typhoon
violent tropical storm or cyclone

vertical columns
upright pillars that help support a building

wrought iron
an easily forged and welded form of iron

INDEX

WEB LINKS

http://science.howstuffworks.com/skyscraper.htm/printable
Learn how skyscrapers fight gravity and wind.

www.skyscraper.org
The Skyscraper Museum in New York hosts virtual tours and skyscraper information on its web site.

http://www.tallestskyscrapers.info/
Learn more about Burj Khalifa, Taipei 101, Petronas Towers, and other skyscrapers.

www.pbs.org/wgbh/buildingbig/lab/forces.html
Watch animations of how different forces can affect a skyscraper.

www.pbs.org/wgbh/buildingbig/skyscraper/basics.html
This web site describes the important basics about skyscrapers.